WORLD ALMANAC® LIBRARY
OF THE
AMERICAN REVOLUTION

Key Battles
of the American Revolution, 1776–1778

Dale Anderson

 WORLD ALMANAC® LIBRARY

Please visit our web site at: www.worldalmanaclibrary.com
For a free color catalog describing World Almanac® Library's list of high-quality books
and multimedia programs, call 1-800-848-2928 (USA) or 1-800-387-3178 (Canada).
World Almanac® Library's fax: (414) 332-3567.

Library of Congress Cataloging-in-Publication Data

Anderson, Dale, 1953-
    Key battles of the American Revolution, 1776-1778 / by Dale Anderson.
        p. cm. — (World Almanac Library of the American Revolution)
    Includes bibliographical references and index.
    ISBN 0-8368-5927-8 (lib. bdg.)
    ISBN 0-8368-5936-7 (softcover)
    1. United States—History—Revolution, 1775-1783—Campaigns—Juvenile literature.
    I. Title. II. Series.
    E230.A53   2005
    973.3'3—dc22   2005040812

First published in 2006 by
World Almanac® Library
A Member of the WRC Media Family of Companies
330 West Olive Street, Suite 100
Milwaukee, WI 53212 USA

Produced by Discovery Books
Editor: Sabrina Crewe
Designer and page production: Sabine Beaupré
Photo researcher: Sabrina Crewe
Maps and diagrams: Stefan Chabluk
Consultant: Andrew Frank, Assistant Professor of History, Florida Atlantic University
World Almanac® Library editorial direction: Mark J. Sachner
World Almanac® Library editor: Alan Wachtel
World Almanac® Library art direction: Tammy West
World Almanac® Library production: Jessica Morris

Photo credits: Brown University Library: pp. 11, 19, 38; CORBIS: cover, pp. 14, 17, 26, 42; Independence National Historical
Park: title page, p. 39; Library of Congress: pp. 5, 21, 34, 41; National Park Service: pp. 30, 32, 37; North Wind Picture Archives:
pp. 7, 9, 13, 22, 25, 35, 43.

Printed in Canada

1 2 3 4 5 6 7 8 9 09 08 07 06 05

*Front cover: This painting by John Trumbull shows the Battle of Princeton on January 3, 1777, during the American
Revolution. The fierce fight gave George Washington's army its first victory over British soldiers on the battlefield.*

*Title page: James Peale painted this portrait of George Washington on horseback in about 1790. He based the
portrait on a work by his brother, Charles Willson Peale—the faces of both the brothers can be seen on the left,
behind Washington. In the background on the right are Revolutionary soldiers, one carrying a French flag.*

Contents

I n 1776, the thirteen British **colonies** along the eastern coast of North America declared themselves independent of Britain. The colonists were already fighting British soldiers in protest at British policies. In 1781, the British surrendered to American forces, and, in 1783, they formally recognized the colonies' independence.

A New Nation

The movement from colonies to independence, known as the American Revolution, gave birth to a new nation—the United States of America. Eventually, the nation stretched to the Pacific Ocean and grew to comprise fifty states. Over time, it was transformed from a nation of farmers into an industrial and technological giant, the world's richest and most powerful country.

An Inspiration to Others

The American Revolution was based on a revolution of ideas. The people who led the American Revolution believed that the purpose of government was to serve the people, not the reverse. They rejected rule by monarchs and created in its place a **republic**. The founders of the republic later wrote a **constitution** that set up this form of government and guaranteed people's basic rights, including the right to speak their minds and the freedom to worship as they wished.

The ideals on which the United States of America was founded have inspired people all around the world ever since. Within a few years of the American Revolution, the people of France had risen up against their monarchy. Over time, the people of colonies in Central

In the summer of 1776, the British returned from Canada to New York City. After defeating the Patriots in a series of battles, they occupied New York in September 1776 and held it until the end of the American Revolution. This picture shows British troops marching into the city.

and South America, in Asia, and in Africa followed the U.S. example and rebelled against their position as colonists. Many former colonies have become independent nations.

The War Begins

The road to the revolution began in the 1760s, when many colonists protested taxes imposed on them by the British government. These protests produced harsh British responses, which prompted yet more protest.

Tension and mutual hostility led to war in the spring of 1775. News of British troops shooting at colonists roused even more people against the government. In June 1775, the British won a victory in a battle outside Boston, but the **Patriots** put up a good fight. After being held under

siege for many months, the British finally left Boston in March 1776, sailing to a temporary base in Canada. The Patriots' military commander in chief, George Washington, knew that the British would return to fight again. The question was where.

Deciding Our Destiny

"My brave fellows . . . your country is at stake: your wives, your houses, and all that you hold dear. You have worn yourselves out with fatigues and hardships, but we know not how to spare you . . . the present is emphatically the crisis which is to decide our destiny."

George Washington addressing his troops, 1776

CHAPTER ONE

The Two Sides

In July 1776, when the colonies declared independence from Britain, they formed the United States of America. The prospects for the new nation, however, seemed slim. It had a population of only 2.5 million people. Of that number, about 500,000—around 20 percent— were African American slaves. In addition, about 500,000 Native Americans lived in the region.

A Powerful Opponent

Britain, on the other hand, had a population of about 11 million. The British had the finest navy in the world, with nearly 300 fighting ships. They also had an army of about 45,000 soldiers and the means to enlist more.

When war broke out in 1775, the Americans had to create an army from scratch. Each colony had **militia** troops, and many soldiers had gained fighting experience in the French and Indian War of 1754–1760. The militia units, however, were controlled by individual colonies, and many militiamen were reluctant to fight in other colonies. In addition, the Americans had no fighting ships.

A New Army

In June 1775, the Continental **Congress**—the Patriot leadership in the colonies—addressed this problem by forming the Continental army to fight the British. It appointed George Washington as the army's leader. Washington also became commander in chief of all other Patriot forces.

American Advantages

The Americans did have several advantages. They were fighting for a cause, and that knowledge

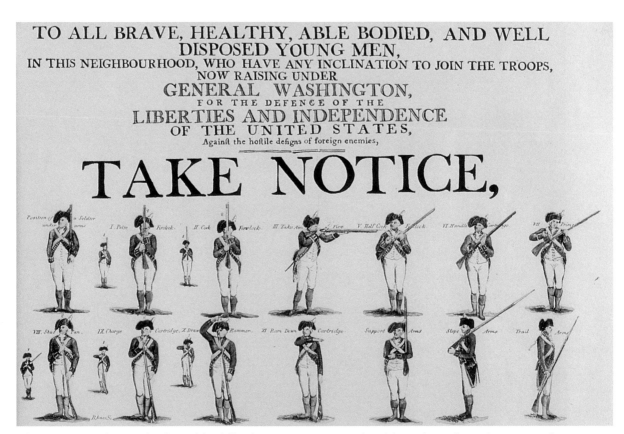

The Continental army had terrible difficulty recruiting enough soldiers throughout the war, with many Americans joining up to fight just for short periods of time. This poster was issued to encourage men to **enlist**.

could inspire their soldiers. They were also battling for their own land, which gave them greater commitment to the effort than British soldiers, who were fighting far from home.

The Patriots also had an easier task than the British. They had only to survive in order to wear the British down. George Washington hoped that, as the conflict dragged on, support for the war in Britain would eventually collapse. He did not have to defeat the British army. He just had to outlast the British will.

George Washington's leadership was another American advantage. Washington was not a perfect general —he constantly complained to the Congress, and his battle plans were almost always too complicated. He was, however, firmly devoted to the cause and provided strong leadership that compelled his officers to act and inspired his men to follow.

American Disadvantages

A major American disadvantage was the presence of Native Americans

African American Soldiers

Most white Americans feared that if African American slaves were armed, they would escape to freedom or stage a slave revolt. The Patriots, therefore, did not recruit blacks—free or enslaved—for the Continental army at first. This decision was made even though some African Americans had fought in New England militia units early in the war. The Americans, however, changed their policy toward enlisting blacks in the face of a severe lack of white troops. In the end, several thousand African Americans served in both the American and British armies. Many who fought with the Americans were granted their freedom, as were some who fought on the British side. A few blacks who helped on either side were sent back into slavery.

who supported the British. Indians living in and to the west of the original thirteen colonies knew that if the Americans won independence, white settlers would soon take their lands. Some Native peoples did side with the Patriots, but most joined the British if they fought at all.

Another major problem was the need for money to supply and feed the army and to create a navy. The Congress had to do this without any source of funds—it could not compel the states to give money because there was no way to enforce such rulings.

Nor could the Congress count on all Americans to join in the effort. Hundreds of thousands of people remained loyal to Britain, and many even fought on the British side. In

addition, the Patriots were, at least at the beginning of the war, unsupported by other nations in their struggle.

British Advantages

Britain had a well-equipped, well-trained army, and its powerful navy could control the oceans and easily move ground forces from one area to another. As a result, the British could conduct operations in more than one place at a time. They also had the financial resources to carry on the fight.

British Disadvantages

The British had disadvantages, too. Crossing the Atlantic Ocean between Britain and America took weeks, causing delays in communication. The British also suffered division at home.

An American militiaman perches in a tree to take a shot at British soldiers during the American Revolution. Although they were short of military equipment and experience, the Patriots were fighting on familiar ground and often in wild areas where the British were vulnerable.

wild terrain made it impossible for the British to do so, whereas Patriot forces took advantage of such terrain to beat them in battle.

Finally, the British faced an overwhelming difficulty. They could not simply defeat Americans in the military sense. Britain wanted to overcome people's hearts and minds and so win back their allegiance as British subjects and colonists. That would, in the end, prove to be an impossible task.

Opponents of the government argued against the war and criticized the government's conduct. The rising cost of the war became an issue.

The British also had a military disadvantage. They were trained to fight in mass movements of troops moving in straight lines to deliver overpowering **bayonet** attacks. When the British could fight that way, they usually won. Often, however, rough ground and

Notions of Liberty

"It is impossible to beat the notion of liberty out of these people. It is rooted in 'em from childhood."

Thomas Gage, commander of British forces in North America at the beginning of the American Revolution

9

CHAPTER TWO

The British Take New York

When the British army evacuated Boston in March 1776, Washington had to figure out his next step. He guessed, correctly, that British commander General William Howe would set his sights on New York City. At the end of March, therefore, Washington started moving his army from Boston to New York.

The British Plan

On July 2, 1776, General Howe began landing thousands of troops on Staten Island in New York Harbor. The British planned to cut New England off from the rest of the colonies because they believed that New England was the hotbed of the Revolution. If the rebellion could be suppressed there, they believed, anger elsewhere would die out.

The British had nearly 24,500 men ready for combat. In addition, General Howe's brother, Admiral Richard Howe, had dozens of ships carrying over 1,000 cannons that could be used to batter Patriot positions.

Washington's Defenses on Long Island

Washington had had plenty of time to prepare his defenses. He could not be sure where the British would strike first, however, so he put soldiers in several places. The largest forces were on Long Island, where they could use cannons to block the British **fleet** from sailing up the East River. Continental army general Nathanael Greene commanded about 4,000 troops at Brooklyn Heights. Another force of nearly equal size held the Heights of Guan, hills farther south.

Defeat on Long Island

In August 1776, General Howe finally moved his massive army from Staten Island. On August 22–25, the British landed large numbers of troops— fifteen to twenty thousand of them— on the southern tip of Long Island. On August 27, they assaulted the Heights of Guan. Two arms of the British army swung around the far right and left of the American lines, encircling the Continental army.

The Defense of Fort Moultrie

While General Howe planned his moves in the North, two other British generals were leading British forces in the South. In May 1776, Henry Clinton and Charles Cornwallis joined forces to plan an attack on Charleston, South Carolina, an important port. Washington sent one of his generals, Charles Lee, to lead the Patriots in defense of the city. On June 28, British warships attacked the city's log fort that stood on Sullivan's Island in Charleston Harbor. The fort's defenders fought back bravely, forcing the British to retreat with over two hundred **casualties**. The fort was later named Fort Moultrie after its commander during the battle, William Moultrie. The defeat at Fort Moultrie discouraged the British from any serious attacks in the South for more than two years.

Sergeant William Jasper raises up Fort Moultrie's fallen flag in the face of enemy fire.

Running from Fire

"The Rebels abandoned every spot as fast, I should say faster, than the King's troops advanced upon them. One of their officers . . . did indeed make an effort to form a considerable line of them in a ploughed field; but they had scarce formed when down came the troops upon the ground, and the poltroons [cowards] ran in the most broken disgraceful and precipitate manner at the very first fire."

Ambrose Serle, secretary to William Howe, journal entry, August 27, 1776

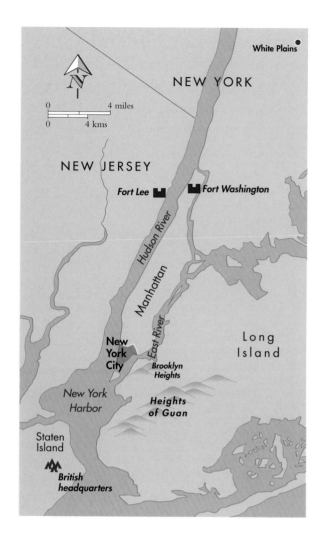

Many battles took place in the area around New York City (shown right) in 1776. Washington and his Continental army had many defeats. The Americans were pushed farther out of the city and eventually into New Jersey.

Fighting was fierce for a few hours, but the Patriots were doomed. About a thousand were taken prisoner, and perhaps half that number were killed and wounded in what became known as the Battle of Long Island. The rest escaped back to Brooklyn Heights.

Howe's plan had been shrewd, and his officers and men had executed it perfectly. He now faced a much reduced force at Brooklyn Heights, one that was demoralized by defeat and retreat. He only had to reach out and crush it, as many of his officers urged. But he waited.

On the night of August 29–30, 1776, under cover of a fierce rain storm, Washington pulled his remaining troops off Long Island and back to Manhattan. When the British awoke the next morning, the Americans were gone.

A Rejected Offer

One reason Howe had waited before attacking was that his brother had instructions to offer Patriot leaders a pardon from the king if they agreed to rejoin Britain. On September 11, 1776, three Patriots—John Adams, Benjamin Franklin, and Edward Rutledge—met Admiral Richard Howe on Staten Island. The admiral made his offer, which the Patriots immediately rejected.

More Patriot Defeats

Washington decided his army's position in Manhattan was too precarious. But before he could pull the army out, General Howe attacked on September 15. The Patriots retreated, and the British occupied New York City.

Fighting a Defensive War

"On our side, the war should be defensive. . . . We should on all occasions avoid a general action, and never be drawn into a necessity to put anything at risk."

George Washington speaking to the Congress, September 1776

The Battle of Long Island on August 27, 1776, was a terrible defeat for the Patriots. This picture shows them retreating after the battle.

Nathan Hale (1755–1776)

Nathan Hale became an early hero of the American cause. A graduate of Yale College, he was a schoolteacher when the war broke out. Hale served with the Connecticut militia during the siege of Boston and moved south with the army to New York early in 1776, where he was given command of a company. Hale volunteered to spy on the British positions on Long Island and was captured in September, just before returning to Patriot lines. Realizing Hale was a spy, General Howe ordered his execution. Before he was hanged on September 22, 1776, the young soldier gave a patriotic speech that ended with the words, "I regret that I have but one life to lose for my country."

Nathan Hale, in the guise of a schoolteacher, spies on British movements.

Afraid of being attacked from the rear, Washington moved north to White Plains at the end of October 1776. The British met the Patriot forces there on October 28 and won another decisive victory. Once more, Washington was forced to flee.

The Continental army then suffered two major losses. They had built a pair of forts to command passage of the Hudson River: Fort Washington near the northern tip of Manhattan and Fort Lee in New Jersey. On November 16, 1776, British soldiers forced the surrender of Fort Washington, taking nearly 3,000 troops prisoner. The Patriots also lost almost 150 cannons. Days later, on November 19, the British moved against Fort Lee. Nathanael Greene

Broken All to Pieces

"[The Continental] army is broken all to pieces, and the spirits of their leaders and their abettors is also broken. However, I think one may venture to pronounce that it is well nigh over with them. All their strongholds are in the hands of his Majesty's troops. All their cannon and mortars, and the greatest part of their stores, ammunition, etc., are gone."

Robert Auchmuty, reporting to Britain after the captures of Forts Washington and Lee, 1776

was able to evacuate with his troops before the British arrived, but he had to leave behind weapons and supplies.

On the Run

Washington fled south through New Jersey, with General Cornwallis in hot pursuit. By December 11, 1776, the Patriots were crossing the Delaware River into Pennsylvania. Fearing the British would soon reach Philadelphia, the Congress left the city December 12 and fled to Baltimore.

Lake Champlain

The Patriots, meanwhile, had suffered another defeat. Retreating from a failed invasion of Canada in summer 1776, Patriot commander Benedict Arnold stopped near Lake Champlain in northern New York to gather his troops. When Arnold learned that the British were building a fleet at a fort upriver from the lake, he also started building one.

By fall 1776, both small fleets were ready. Arnold, hoping to surprise the British, led fifteen boats to a sheltered spot on the western side of the lake. The British, however, found and battered the American ships. The Patriots lost several vessels in a fierce fight at Valcour Island on October 11 and the rest two days later. Arnold and a fraction of his force escaped to safety at Fort Ticonderoga, but the British controlled the lake.

CHAPTER THREE

Washington Fights Back

By late December 1776, the Americans' position looked awful. The British held New York City, and the Congress had been forced to flee from Philadelphia. After a series of losses on the battlefield and several retreats, the Continental army—just a tiny, disheartened shadow of its earlier self—was huddling in the cold in Pennsylvania, with only the Delaware River protecting it from a British attack. Washington's small army was about to get even smaller. When the year ran out, so would the enlistment period of many of his soldiers.

The British Winter Camps

Meanwhile, Howe had decided to put his men in winter quarters. He kept the main body of troops in New York City. He stationed smaller **garrisons** at bases in New Jersey to keep hold of areas that Washington had abandoned. Those troops who were camped in New Jersey at Trenton and Bordentown were just across the river from the Continental army in Pennsylvania. Scattered as it was, the British army was vulnerable to attack.

Desperate for a victory—especially before he lost more of his soldiers—Washington decided to prepare an offensive against the British at Trenton, where 1,500 German **mercenary** soldiers were stationed. The attack would come early in the

General Washington (standing, left) leads his troops back into New Jersey across the freezing Delaware River in December 1776.

morning of December 26, 1776, the day after Christmas. The Germans had a reputation for celebrating Christmas with great enthusiasm and much liquor. Washington believed he would find them unprepared to fight the morning after.

Attack on Trenton

On Christmas night, in an icy storm, Washington took 2,400 soldiers in rowboats across the Delaware River from Pennsylvania to New Jersey, landing a few miles north of Trenton.

Trying Times

"These are the times that try men's souls. The summer soldier and the sunshine patriot will in this crisis shrink from the service of their country; but he that stands it now deserves the love and thanks of man and woman. Tyranny, like Hell, is not easily conquered; yet we have this consolation with us, that the harder the conflict, the more glorious the triumph."

Writer Thomas Paine, from The Crisis, *a series of essays written to inspire soldiers and other Patriots, December 1776*

17

Time Off for Winter

Warfare in the 1700s was not a full-time affair. The fighting season was limited largely to the spring and summer, with some operations in the fall. Winter, with its cold and snow, was thought to be no fit time for marching and fighting. Late in the year, therefore, commanders put their men in winter quarters. Soldiers liked the arrangement because it gave them a few months in the year to rest.

Marching south, the men reached the outskirts of Trenton early in the morning on December 26.

At 8:00 A.M., the Patriot attack began. The Germans awoke from their sleep and started to defend themselves, but American **artillery** quickly overcame them. After just an hour or so of fighting, the German soldiers surrendered.

Washington had won his victory. At a cost of a handful of wounded men—including future president James Monroe—he had captured over 900 enemy soldiers and left at least 100 dead and wounded.

Howe Sends More Troops

Howe responded immediately, sending 5,500 troops under General Charles Cornwallis from New York toward Princeton, New Jersey. Meanwhile, Washington persuaded a group of militiamen from New England to stay

on in the Continental army by making a stirring speech and offering a $10 bonus to soldiers who stayed.

On January 2, 1777, Cornwallis's army arrived. Washington was trapped east of Trenton between the British and the river. Some British officers urged an immediate attack, but Cornwallis thought the next day would be soon enough.

Saved by Cornwallis's decision to delay, the Continental army escaped. Shortly after midnight on January 3,

Waiting Until Morning

"We've got the old fox [Washington] safe now. We'll go over and bag him in the morning."

General Cornwallis, deciding not to attack the Continental army, January 2, 1777

The Battle of Princeton in January 1777 was short but ferocious. It ended in a much-needed victory for the Continental army.

Washington moved most of his army out of camp. A few hundred men stayed behind until morning to tend the campfires and make it appear that the whole army was still there. The British slept soundly, not realizing that the Americans had escaped.

Washington Wins Again

That same day, January 3, Washington marched his men north toward New Brunswick, New Jersey, an important British supply depot. On the way there, they ran into British forces near Princeton. In a brief fight, the Americans suffered only about forty casualties, while the British reported over three hundred.

After the Battle of Princeton, Washington led his soldiers to Morristown, New Jersey, where they established winter quarters. The defeats at Trenton and Princeton forced Cornwallis to retreat to New Brunswick, where the British army, too, settled in for the winter.

Fighting Near Philadelphia

O n July 23, 1777, General William Howe sailed from New York City with 15,000 men. His goal was to capture Philadelphia, where the Congress had resumed its meetings.

Moving to Pennsylvania

Howe hoped to find large numbers of **Loyalists** in Philadelphia who would help the British cause. He knew, for instance, that many Quakers in the city, being antiwar, did not support the Patriots.

When Howe left New York City, Washington marched his army out of New Jersey. He guessed, correctly, that Howe would try to take Philadelphia next. In August, he learned that Howe was landing his troops at the head of Chesapeake Bay, southwest of the city. Soon after, Washington positioned nearly 11,000 troops along Brandywine Creek, between the British army and Philadelphia.

Confusing Fords

Washington chose Brandywine Creek because it was deep enough that the British would need to use **fords** to cross it. The decision was a sound one, except that the creek had so many fords that the British had several choices for places to cross. Those options made Washington's defense more difficult. On top of that, the Americans did not have an accurate count of all the fords, and

Founded by Quakers, Philadelphia was the largest city in the new United States of America. Its capture was an important victory for the British.

commanders in different parts of the field did not all use the same names to refer to them. During the Battle of Brandywine, these facts would cause confusing reports that almost led to the destruction of Washington's army.

Quakers in the American Revolution

Members of the Society of Friends (also called Quakers) believe everyone has a direct relationship with God without the need for priests or ministers. Quakers believe in the equality of all people and are opposed to war under any circumstances. Their beliefs set them apart from other Christian churches in the 1600s and 1700s. To avoid persecution, Quakers established the colony of Pennsylvania in 1682.

Quakers were against the increasing violence of the Revolution rather than against the Patriot cause. As the war progressed, large numbers of Quakers remained loyal to the British for this reason. Quakers did not join either army, except for a few—including a breakaway group known as the "Free Quakers"—who decided to fight for independence. Many Quaker families in Philadelphia housed British officers during the army's occupation of the city in 1777 and 1778. They paid the price that other Loyalists paid, losing their homes and going into exile when the British left Philadelphia.

A Hot Evening

"At half after four o'clock, the enemy attacked General Sullivan . . . above this [position], and the action has been very violent ever since. It still continues. A very severe cannonade has [begun] here too, and I suppose we shall have a very hot evening."

George Washington, message to the Congress during the Battle of Brandywine, 1777

The Americans held their positions as long as they could at the Battle of Brandywine on September 11, 1777. They had to retreat, however, when they were overwhelmed by the British.

The Battle of Brandywine

Howe's plan called for the same kind of move he had made at Long Island the year before. One force would create a diversion by attacking the center of Washington's line, at a place called Chadd's Ford. Meanwhile, General Cornwallis would lead a large force around the right side of the American

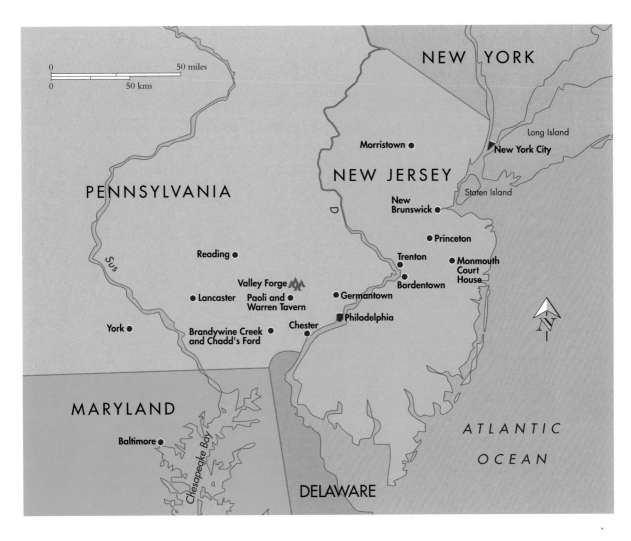

British forces had several victories in the fighting around Philadelphia in the summer and fall of 1777. The British eventually secured the city.

line and then attack the enemy from the rear.

The attack on Chadd's Ford began early in the morning on September 11, 1777. Washington realized the attacking force was not the entire British army and wondered where the rest was. Rumors reached him during the day of British soldiers to the north and west—beyond the right side of his line. When the general tried to have the reports confirmed, however, his scouts said they saw no one. Late in the afternoon, Washington realized that the British had come around his right and were now behind his lines.

Defense and Retreat

Washington quickly put together a stout defense, but the oncoming British troops were too numerous. Washington ordered a retreat. He

Anthony Wayne (1745–1796)

Nicknamed "Mad Anthony" for his boldness, Anthony Wayne was born in Pennsylvania. He worked as a **surveyor** and was a business owner. Active in the Pennsylvania **legislature** before the war, Wayne became a militia colonel. He reached the rank of general by 1777 and took part in several of the battles around Philadelphia. After the surprise attack at Paoli, there were rumors that Wayne had failed in his leadership. To clear his name of any blame, Wayne requested a **court-martial**. The court ruled that he had not neglected his duty, and Wayne was able to return to service. He fought in several other battles until the end of the war, when he retired. Wayne was called back to the army in 1792 and took charge of a force sent to fight Native Americans in Ohio. Wayne won the Battle of Fallen Timbers near Toledo in 1794, a victory that enabled the United States to seize large amounts of Native American land in Ohio for white settlers.

was able to pull his men out and retire to the town of Chester, closer to Philadelphia and still between the city and the British.

Once more, Howe had out-maneuvered Washington. The British army had fewer than 600 killed and wounded soldiers. The Americans had over 1,200 casualties, including 400 who had been taken prisoner. Once more, however, Washington had managed to escape Howe's trap.

Bayonet Attack

After a **skirmish** on September 16 at Warren Tavern, Washington pulled his troops back east toward Philadelphia,

leaving one division under General Anthony Wayne as a rear guard. Wayne's men were stationed at the village of Paoli in Pennsylvania. On the night of September 21, a British force surprised them in their sleep. The British used their bayonets to stab many of the startled Americans. Wayne gathered his forces quickly and was able to escape with the vast majority of his force, but he lost well over 100 soldiers.

The British in Philadelphia

Over the next few days, Howe continued to trick Washington. He sent his army toward the north, away

Dreadful Scene

"The enemy . . . some with arms, others without, [ran] in all directions with the greatest confusion. The light infantry bayoneted every man they came up with. The camp was immediately set on fire, and this, with the cries of the wounded, formed altogether one of the most dreadful scenes I ever beheld."

British officer, report on the attack at Paoli, 1777

Anthony Wayne stands beside his horse in camp during the American Revolution.

from Philadelphia. Washington, who was puzzled by this change of course, concluded that Howe was aiming for the city of Reading, an important supply point for the Continental army. Washington, therefore, pointed his army in that direction. But while Washington headed north, Howe turned his army around and took it into Philadelphia. On September 26, 1777, the city fell into British hands without a fight.

New Recruits

In the preceding month, Washington's army had been defeated at the Battle of Brandywine and outmaneuvered around Philadelphia. Washington had

General Howe was commander in chief of the British army in America from October 1775 to April 1778. During that time, he captured the two main U.S. cities and defeated the Patriots in many battles.

seen his army cut in half by battle losses, illness, and desertion. The general, however, had one more card to play: reinforcements were arriving. By early October 1777, Washington again had a force of about 11,000 men. He was determined to use them.

The Battle of Germantown

Howe's force, meanwhile, was split into several parts. Some troops were being used to ensure the flow of supplies from the Chesapeake Bay to Philadelphia. Others were attacking American-held forts on the Delaware River. Howe had two main bodies of troops—one in Philadelphia and another to the north, in the area around Germantown.

Washington decided to strike at the Germantown force, which numbered about 9,000 men. He had a highly

Revolutionary Capitals

The British capture of Philadelphia forced the Continental Congress to flee for the second time. The Congress had left Philadelphia for Baltimore the previous December, but the leaders had returned in March 1777 to continue their business of running the new nation and the war. In September, however, the Congress decided that the British were dangerously close once again. On September 19, a week before Howe entered the city, the members of the Congress headed for Lancaster, a town west of Philadelphia. From late September 1777 until late June 1778, the Congress met in York, Pennsylvania.

complicated plan that involved four sections of his army attacking at the same time.

The Patriots made a sudden attack on October 4. The surprise element helped them gain an early advantage, but they ran into problems. In a heavy fog, two Patriot units collided, both thinking they had stumbled upon the enemy. Soldiers fired and ran for the rear in a panic.

In the end, Washington had to retreat—he had lost more than a thousand men, over four hundred of them taken prisoner by the British.

Curiously, the failed battle lifted American spirits. The soldiers believed that they had almost won it. And they liked the boldness that their usually cautious commander had shown. After weeks of hardship and defeat, Washington had attacked.

In Good Spirits

"From the bravery, and, I may add, the discipline, of our troops, much may be expected. In the late engagement they did their duty, maintaining the action upwards of two hours and a half, teaching themselves and the world this useful truth, founded on experience, that British troops are proof against neither a surprise nor a vigorous attack. . . . Our army is now encamped in a good part of the country, about twenty-six miles from Philadelphia, [and] is in good spirits."

Patriot soldier Samuel Shaw, letter to his father after the Battle of Germantown, October 1777

CHAPTER FIVE

Victory at Saratoga

Away from Philadelphia, there were other developments in 1777. Back in February, the British general John Burgoyne had presented an ambitious plan to the British government. His plan was to seize control of all of New York in order to split New England from the rest of the country and so weaken the Patriots.

Burgoyne's Plan

The plan called for a large army to march south from Canada along Lake Champlain and the Hudson River. Meanwhile, another, smaller force of British and Native Americans troops would move west from the Great Lakes toward the Hudson River, eliminating American forts along the way. Yet a third force under General Howe would march north from New York City. The combined force would meet at Albany, New York, and then sweep east into New England and crush the Revolution. George Germain, the British secretary of state for the colonies, approved the plan and put Burgoyne in charge of the force moving from Canada.

The Campaign Begins

Burgoyne launched his campaign in the middle of June 1777. He had nearly eight thousand men, including some Canadians and a few hundred Native Americans as well as British and German soldiers. A confident Burgoyne issued a proclamation on June 23, promising peace for loyal subjects but severe punishment for Patriots.

Burgoyne had a victory on July 6, seizing Fort Ticonderoga on Lake Champlain. After that, however, Burgoyne's men advanced at a

Burgoyne's Supply Train

Rough country and trees felled by American axes made the British advance difficult. The **infantry** could have overcome these obstacles if marching alone, but the soldiers' difficulties were made acute by the size of Burgoyne's supply train. It carried many dozens of cannons, which Burgoyne insisted would be needed to attack Patriot forces. The supply wagons also carried large quantities of personal effects—extra uniforms, special food, and fine wine—for the senior officers. Thirty carts were needed to haul Burgoyne's personal supplies alone. A German officer with some experience had warned of this problem in advance. To move through the forest, he had said, an army "must be almost without baggage." British officers, however, paid little attention to the advice of German officers.

snail's pace through New York's forest. They were marching through very difficult terrain, an area with steep mountains, deep valleys, and no roads except Indian paths. To cross those valleys, the army had to build bridges, and each bridge took time. To slow British progress even more, Patriots cut down trees along the route and dropped boulders into creeks to block boats. The British only moved 22 miles (35 kilometers) in nearly three weeks.

Two British Defeats

While Burgoyne's men struggled south, another British army was having trouble, too. Burgoyne's plan had called for a smaller British force to

move down the Mohawk River valley to capture Patriot-held forts there and march to the Hudson River. Early in August 1777, that army—under General Barry St. Leger—was unable

Messengers of Justice and Wrath

"The messengers of justice and of wrath await [Patriots] in the field, and devastation, famine, and every concomitant horror . . . will bar the way to their return."

General John Burgoyne, Proclamation, June 23, 1777

to capture Fort Stanwix, just east of Lake Oneida. St. Leger kept his army in the area, however, hoping to force the garrison at the fort to surrender.

The Patriots sent two relief forces to help their soldiers at Fort Stanwix. The first was ambushed at nearby Oriskany by Mohawk leader Joseph Brant and his warriors. The second, under Benedict Arnold, reached the fort on August 22. St. Leger then decided that his army could not

oppose the combined Patriot forces and pulled back to Canada. One part of Burgoyne's plan was now in ashes. The proposed army from New York City, meanwhile, had failed to appear because Howe was busy with his campaign to take Philadelphia.

The next British defeat came to the east. Burgoyne sent a force of British and German troops to capture some supplies from Patriot stores at Bennington, in what is now Vermont.

Fort Stanwix, originally a French trading post, was rebuilt in 1758 by British general John Stanwix. It was renamed Fort Schuyler by the Patriots when they took it over during the Revolution. The building that stands on the site of Fort Stanwix today, shown here, is a replica of the fort as it was in the 1770s.

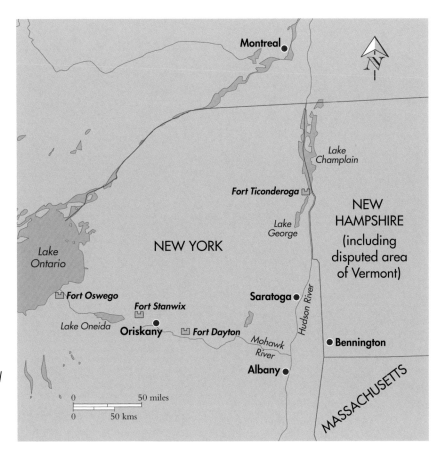

In mid-1777, the war spread north from the Philadelphia and New York City areas to northern New York.

On August 16, near Bennington, Burgoyne's troops ran into a body of Patriot militia nearly twice their number. The result was a complete American victory. The militia suffered about 50 casualties, while the British had more than 200 dead and around 700 taken prisoner.

The Americans Gather

Burgoyne's slow advance was just what the Patriots needed. Outrage over Burgoyne's June proclamation and several violent Native American attacks had combined to attract many Americans to the Patriot cause. By mid-September, Continental army general Horatio Gates had about 7,000 men in the region. Burgoyne had about the same number, but most of his Native Americans had left him. He had relied on them for scouting and had no idea, therefore, where Gates's army was.

At Saratoga

By mid-September 1777, Burgoyne finally reached an area south of Saratoga and north of Albany. He found that Gates was nearby with his men, dug in on high ground. On the morning of September 19, Burgoyne

History enthusiasts stage a reenactment of the fighting at Saratoga on the original battlefield, now a national historical monument. This photo shows Patriots attacking a British position.

Deadly Fire

"A little after 12 our advanced pickets came up [to the Americans under] Colonel Morgan and engaged [the enemy], but from the great superiority of fire received from him . . . they were obliged to fall back, every officer being either killed or wounded except one."

British soldier William Digby, journal entry on the First Battle of Saratoga, 1777

sent his troops forward, hoping to draw the Americans into a fight. Patriot riflemen opened fire, targeting British officers first. Their fierce attack sent the first troops scattering.

The day's action centered on an area of cleared farmland. Whichever side gained the clearing was subjected to withering fire from the other side hidden in the woods. After those in the clearing would retreat, their opponents would surge into the space and then suffer heavy casualties themselves. After a long day of seesaw fighting, the battle ended in a draw.

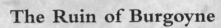

The Ruin of Burgoyne

"We have taken thirty prisoners since the battle, and as many more deserted. Our men are in fine spirits, [and] are very bold and daring. . . . Matters can't remain long as they now are. Burgoyne has only twenty days' provision. He must give us battle in a day or two, or else retire back. . . . In either case, I think, with the blessing of heaven, he must be ruined."

American soldier John Glover, letter to a relative in Massachusetts, September 29, 1777

The armies remained in the area after the battle, both sides digging in. The British soldiers were living on nothing more than flour and salt pork, and many were deserting. Constant American raids kept the British on edge and largely without sleep. Gates, meanwhile, had received reinforcements and had more than 11,000 men.

The Second Battle of Saratoga

On October 7, Burgoyne once again advanced his forces to probe the Patriot lines on Bemis Heights. Once more, American riflemen positioned themselves in the woods on either side of the advancing British and peppered them with fire. The Patriot forces eventually overwhelmed the British and drove them back.

Patriot general Benedict Arnold then appeared on the scene. He pushed the Patriots forward to capture a few hundred British troops in one of their **redoubts**. The battle ended with only about 150 American casualties. The British losses were four times higher and included two able generals.

Burgoyne's Surrender

Burgoyne withdrew to Saratoga. Finding himself surrounded by a force three times the size of his own, he offered to surrender. Gates agreed that the British forces could be paroled, meaning they would not be taken as prisoners but had to promise not to fight again during the current war.

The formal surrender took place on October 17, 1777. Gates entertained Burgoyne and the top British officers at a dinner while Burgoyne's men laid down their arms and marched away. The Americans had deprived the British of nearly 5,000 troops and just as many guns. It was a sorry end to Burgoyne's campaign.

A Diplomatic Victory

The American success at Saratoga led to another triumph. Word of Burgoyne's surrender reached France in early December 1777. At the end of the previous year, the Congress had sent Benjamin Franklin and two other **diplomats** to France to seek the aid the Patriots so desperately needed.

33

British soldiers lay down their arms during the surrender ceremony at Saratoga. It was this Patriot victory that persuaded France to support the Americans' struggle for independence.

The French had, until this time, resisted American pleas. They had been reluctant to join the Patriots in a lost cause, but the news from Saratoga tipped the scales. The attraction for France was simple: a U.S. victory would weaken Britain, France's long-time rival.

On December 17, the French informed the American diplomats in Paris that they recognized the United States as an independent nation. Although a formal **treaty** was not signed until February 1778, the United States had won an important and much-needed ally.

Benjamin Franklin in Paris

The United States could not have had a more perfect representative in France than Benjamin Franklin. Before the Revolutionary War, Franklin was undoubtedly the most famous American, well known abroad for his writings and his scientific experiments. The French were ready to celebrate his arrival in their country, and Franklin's wit and charm helped confirm their high opinion. Franklin's writings were translated into French and published over and over again. Artists clamored to paint his portrait, and their images were turned into black-and-white copies that printers sold to an eager public. One of those proclaimed the French view of Franklin's greatness as an electrical inventor and a fighter for independence. Its caption read, "He seized lightning from the sky and the scepter from tyrants."

Women in Paris wore hats decorated with dangling lightning rods—one of Franklin's many inventions—to express their admiration for the famous American.

CHAPTER SIX

A Long Winter

I n the late fall of 1777, Washington had to confront a challenge to his authority. During the Revolution, Washington was not universally admired by his colleagues. General Charles Lee, who hoped to take over Washington's command, accused him of indecision, which in war was worse than stupidity, he said. Even supporters, such as Nathanael Greene, complained that Washington was not decisive. Johann de Kalb, a German officer in the Continental army, judged the commander in chief "too slow . . . and far too weak." Washington's loss of New York in 1776 and Philadelphia in 1777 did nothing to win him a reputation as a skilled general.

Doubts in the Congress

Some members of the Congress were also unhappy with Washington. A few feared he was gaining too much power and influence, while others said he was too lenient with Loyalists. Many in the Congress had also grown tired of Washington's letters and reports, which were famous for their laments about everything from the inexperience of the militia and shortage of supplies to his lack of support from the Congress.

Late in 1777, these doubts caused the Congress to create a committee that had the power to oversee Washington's decisions. Several people on the committee opposed Washington. Meanwhile, critical comments about him written by a fellow general, Thomas Conway, became known.

Many other officers, however, rose to their commander's defense, and the Congress was forced to realize that, if they lost Washington,

Visitors to the site of the Continental army camp at Valley Forge can now see replicas of the cabins built by the soldiers in the winter of 1777–1778.

they might lose most of the army's officer corps. General Conway lost all his support and was forced out of the army. The commander in chief, meanwhile, emerged in a strengthened position.

A Bitter Winter

While Washington dealt with these challenges, he also settled his army into winter quarters at Valley Forge, northwest of Philadelphia. The camp

Barefoot Army

"It is certain that half the army are naked, and almost the whole army go barefoot. . . . The men have had neither meat nor bread for four days, and our horses are often left without any fodder. What will be done when the roads grow worse, and the season more severe?"

Patriot general Johann de Kalb, letter describing conditions at Valley Forge, December 1777

was on high ground, there was plenty of fresh water, and the surrounding forests provided ample wood for building shelters and making fires. But the pitiful army lacked everything else, including food, shoes, clothing, and housing.

Within about a month of arrival, Washington's soldiers had built cabins to live in. The food problem, however, was not solved so quickly. Farmers in Pennsylvania carried their produce to Philadelphia, where the British paid them gold and silver. The farmers refused to sell their food to the Continental army in exchange for promises of future payment. And Washington refused to seize the food, fearing such action would alienate people. Most soldiers, therefore, lived on nothing but "firecakes"—flour and water mixed and "baked" on hot rocks. Sometimes even those ran out. Clothes and shoes were also impossible to find.

A print shows George Washington and his wife Martha visiting the troops at Valley Forge on Christmas Day, 1777. What it doesn't show is that many of the troops were freezing, barefoot, and had only rags to cover them.

Friedrich von Steuben (1730–1794)

Baron Friedrich Wilhelm Augustus von Steuben was something of a fraud. He called himself a German general, but he had never held that rank. He might not have been a baron either, and some historians believe his reputation as the expert who drilled discipline into the Continental army is a bit exaggerated. Still, the colorful soldier unquestionably helped the American cause.

Von Steuben joined the Prussian army in his late teens, serving until he was dismissed many years later, in 1763. In 1777, he arrived in Paris, in debt and needing a job. There he obtained an introduction to Benjamin Franklin, who sent the German off to America. Von Steuben eventually joined Washington's staff and began training the army. Washington was clearly pleased by the results and asked the Congress to promote the German to major general. After the war, von Steuben became an American citizen and retired to New York.

The Situation Improves

By February 1778, the situation at Valley Forge improved. Washington put Nathanael Greene in charge of getting food and supplies. Greene acted with energy, sending healthy soldiers to Delaware, New Jersey, and Maryland to obtain food. Uniforms and shoes arrived, and, with food and clothing, the soldiers' spirits perked up.

Another timely event was the arrival of German officer Friedrich von Steuben, who introduced a training program for the soldiers. Von Steuben barked out the orders in French, and an American officer translated them into English. Von Steuben also wrote a booklet spelling out the proper techniques for attacking in formation, loading and firing a gun,

Starving and Freezing

"I am sick—discontented—and out of humor. Poor food—hard lodging—cold weather—fatigue—nasty clothes—nasty cookery . . . smoked out of my senses . . . I can't endure it—why are we sent here to starve and freeze. . . . Here all confusion—smoke and cold—hunger and flilthyness."

Doctor Albigence Waldo, diary entry from Valley Forge, December 14, 1777

and using a bayonet. This, too, was translated into English, and copies were made for each unit in the army. After weeks of lying around and feeling miserable, the soldiers—now that they had food—actually enjoyed the training. Soon the entire army was learning von Steuben's drills.

The British in Winter

General Howe and other British officers, meanwhile, were having a comfortable winter in Philadelphia. While they enjoyed parties with the local Loyalists, put on plays, and gambled at cards, their soldiers suffered from poor food and water.

Many British officers held Howe responsible for failing to destroy the Continental army. The general, tired of his post, asked to be relieved of command. After much debate, the British government agreed, putting General Sir Henry Clinton in Howe's place in May 1778.

The Carlisle Peace Commission

The British made one last diplomatic effort to end the war. They sent a new peace commission, which arrived in Philadelphia on June 6, 1778. The commissioners, headed by Frederick Howard, the Earl of Carlisle, offered to undo all the laws Britain had passed about the colonies since 1763 and to negotiate with the Congress about America's status. Britain would not recognize U.S. independence, however, and so on June 17, the Congress dismissed the British request for a meeting. Before returning to Britain, the peace commissioners threatened great destruction. They told General Clinton to treat the Americans as an enemy and to pursue them without mercy.

The British Leave Philadelphia

Fearing that France would send a fleet that could trap the British army in Philadelphia, the British government ordered Clinton to leave Philadelphia for New York. Clinton had hoped to depart by sea, but about three thousand Loyalists wanted to leave as well. Unable to move so many people by ship, Clinton had to march overland.

On June 18, 1778, the British began their long march back to New York. Burdened with tons of baggage and a 12-mile (19-km) trail of Loyalists, Clinton's army moved very slowly.

Washington's army, meanwhile, was on the move from Valley Forge and catching up with the British. As his forces got within striking distance of Clinton's army, Washington was itching to try out his newly trained Continental troops. General Charles Lee—his second in command—protested that the Americans could not stand up to British troops. At a council of war, the majority of the senior officers agreed with Lee. Only three—Nathanael Greene, Anthony Wayne, and the young French general the Marquis de Lafayette—urged their commander on. Overruling the majority, Washington decided to attack.

Washington (on the left in the main group) confers with his generals during the Revolutionary War.

"Molly Pitcher"

Legend says that a woman named Mary Ludwig Hays marched in the Continental army along with her husband John, an artilleryman. During the Battle of Monmouth, the story goes, she carried water to him and his comrades, earning her nickname "Molly Pitcher." Later, her husband was wounded or perhaps killed. Mrs. Hays then took his place at the gun. In some versions of the story, a grateful George Washington made her a sergeant after the battle.

But is the story true? No one knows. There are a few reports from people at the battle of a woman who brought water to American soldiers. The other details, however, did not appear until well into the 1800s, long after the battle. It might be that Molly Pitcher was a creation of the public imagination. Or maybe people mistakenly linked the woman at Monmouth with another woman— Margaret Corbin— who did take her husband's position in an artillery team when he was killed during the fighting at Fort Washington, New York, in 1776.

Molly Pitcher loads a cannon at the Battle of Monmouth.

The Continental army fires artillery at British forces in the Battle of Monmouth in June 1778.

The Battle of Monmouth

The two armies met near Monmouth Court House, New Jersey, on June 28, 1778. Washington placed Lee in command out of respect for his rank. Lee's lack of confidence in the plan, however, showed in his performance. He attacked the British, but they beat back the assault and sent Lee and his troops reeling in an uncontrolled retreat with British soldiers close behind.

The retreating soldiers ran into Washington, advancing with the rest of the Continental army. Washington sent the panicked troops to the rear to regroup. He put fresh troops into a defensive line. When the Americans repulsed the leading British units, Clinton threw more forces into the battle, but the American lines held. At dusk, Washington tried to organize a counterattack, but the soldiers—who had been marching and fighting all day in intense heat—could not continue. Late that night, Clinton's army left Monmouth and continued north.

Monmouth—the last major battle of the Revolution in the North— was technically a draw. Washington believed that Lee's retreat had cost the Patriots a great victory. The men of the Continental army, however, had fought better than ever before. There was hope for the future.

They Shall Do It

Charles Lee: "Sir, these troops are not able to meet British **grenadiers**."
George Washington: "Sir, they are able and, by God, they shall do it."

Conversation at the Battle of Monmouth, 1778

Time Line

1776   March 17: British evacuate Boston.
March 18: Continental army starts arriving in New York City area.
June: Patriots defend Fort Moultrie in Charleston Harbor.
July 2: British land on Staten Island.
July 4: Congress approves Declaration of Independence.
August 27: Battle of Long Island.
September 11: Americans reject British peace offer.
October 11–13: Patriot forces suffer defeat on Lake Champlain.
October 28: Battle of White Plains.
November 16: British capture Fort Washington.
November 20: British capture Fort Lee.
December 7: Washington's army reaches safety in Pennsylvania.
December 12: Congress leaves Philadelphia.
December 26: Washington's army captures Trenton from British.

1777   January 3: Washington's army captures Princeton from British.
July 6: General John Burgoyne captures Fort Ticonderoga from Patriots.
August 3: British advance from Great Lakes is halted at Fort Stanwix.
August 16: Patriot militia defeat British near Bennington, Vermont.

August 22: British withdraw from Fort Stanwix.
September 11: British victory at Battle of Brandywine.
September 16: British and Americans skirmish at Warren Tavern.
September 19: Congress leaves Philadelphia; First Battle of Saratoga.
September 21: British bayonet attack at Paoli.
September 26: British capture Philadelphia.
October 4: Battle of Germantown.
October 7: Second Battle of Saratoga.
October 17: British surrender to Patriots at Saratoga.
December 17: France and United States agree to an alliance.
December: Washington's army enters winter quarters at Valley Forge.

1778   February 6: United States and France sign treaty of alliance.
May 8: Henry Clinton takes command of British forces in North America.
June 17: Congress rejects proposal of Carlisle Peace Commission.
June 18: British and Loyalists begin leaving Philadelphia.
June 28: Battle of Monmouth.

Glossary

artillery: large heavy guns, such as cannons.

bayonet: blade attached to front end of a shoulder gun and used to stab the enemy in combat.

casualty: soldier or other person who is wounded, killed, or missing in battle.

colony: settlement, area, or country owned or controlled by another nation.

congress: meeting. The name "Congress" was given to the first meetings of delegates from the British colonies and was then adopted as the name of the U.S. legislature when the United States formed a national government.

constitution: document that lays down the basic rules and laws of a nation or organization.

court-martial: trial of a member of a military force.

diplomat: person who represents his or her country in a foreign country.

enlist: join a military force.

fleet: group of ships under a single command.

ford: shallow spot in water where it is possible to cross.

garrison: military post; or the troops stationed at a military post.

grenadier: member of an especially strong attack force within the British army.

infantry: soldiers who fight on foot.

legislature: group of officials that makes laws.

Loyalist: American who rejected independence and wanted the colonies to remain British.

mercenary: soldier who serves just for money, especially one hired by a foreign country to fight on its behalf.

militia: group of citizens organized into an army (as opposed to an army of professional soldiers, or regulars).

Patriot: American who supported the American Revolution; more generally, a person who is loyal to and proud of his or her country.

redoubt: small fortification, usually built of earth or wood, where artillery was placed to fire at an enemy.

republic: nation that is led by elected officials and that has no monarch.

siege: military operation in which a group of attackers surrounds a target and either attacks it or keeps it trapped in an attempt to force it to surrender.

skirmish: minor fight during a war or before or after a larger battle.

surveyor: person who measures land, works out boundaries, and makes records of information about land.

treaty: agreement made after negotiations among two or more nations or groups.

Further Resources

Books

Ammon, Richard. *Valley Forge.* Holiday House, 2004.

Kneib, Martha. *A Historical Atlas of the American Revolution* (The United States: Historical Atlases of the Growth of a New Nation). Rosen, 2004.

Marrin, Albert. *George Washington and the Founding of a New Nation.* Dutton, 2001.

Murray, Aaron. R. *American Revolution Battles and Leaders.* DK Publishing, 2004.

Schmittroth, Linda. *American Revolution Almanac* (American Revolution Reference Library). UXL, 2000.

Places to Visit

Valley Forge National Historical Park
National Park Service
P.O. Box 953
Valley Forge, PA 19482
Telephone: (610) 783-1077

Web Sites

British Battles
www.britishbattles.com
Web site offering analysis and details of historic battles involving the British army and covering many of the important battles of the American Revolution.

Saratoga National Historical Park
www.nps.gov/sara
National Park Service Web site offers virtual tour of the battlefield at Saratoga and detailed accounts of the battles.

US Presidents—George Washington
www.whitehouse.gov/kids/presidents/ georgewashington.html
White House Web site offers facts about George Washington, including his height, schooling, and favorite foods.

Valley Forge National Historical Park
www.nps.gov/vafo
National Park Service Web site offers maps of sites at Washington's winter camp together with images and historical information.

Index